# WITH NO REGRETS

## Getting Older:
## Face It, Live It, Love It

By Jane H. Goldman

*Illustrated by Lauren Martin*

ISBN: 978-0-578-54845-6

The Three Tomatoes Publishing
New York
www.thethreetomatoes.com

Cover Photo: iStock

Cover Graphics: Susan Herbst

Internal Illustrations: Lauren Martin

# DEDICATION

To my sister Susan Rahn who didn't have enough tomorrows, her children Robert and Peter Martin, their wives, Lauren and Annie, and to Susan's grand-children Todd, Dan, Lauren, William, James, Lily, and Evan, for all their many tomorrows.

## JUST ONE MORE

Ask me about my "Bucket List"

In a world of "Been there, done that"


The list is a simple one

One line, one ask


Each day I strike it out

Then write it in again


A simple request

"Tomorrow"

# Table of Contents

# PREFACE

Many years ago, I started writing short pieces about life—often how I was feeling about mine at any given time, or what my friends were feeling about theirs— whether it was about growing older, relationships, careers, friendships, and loss. Basically, the stuff of life. Other pieces were my somewhat quirky observations about life.

For many of those years, my writings were a way for my right brain to exercise itself as my left brain did most of the work as a corporate attorney by day.

Sometimes I would read pieces to my friends and they liked them. Sometimes they laughed, sometimes they nodded in agreement of feelings mutually shared. So these stories represent all of our stories

Recently at the urging of some friends, I decided to turn them into a book of reflections. I have to say, it's scary to put your thoughts out there to the world. But I hope in doing so, that some of you will laugh and nod and see yourself in this journey of life too.

With gratitude,

Jane H. Goldman

# WHERE DID I GO?

I look in the mirror and try to find myself. But I can't. Where did I go?

I remember the first shocking time I suddenly noticed that I couldn't recognize myself. It was Christmas, looking at a department store's decorated window and seeing a reflection of a strange woman staring back at me who just wasn't me.

Then only last month, while in a ladies' room, I saw several young women's faces reflected in the mirrors, combing their hair like I was. They left. I was standing there alone, but it was my image they took with them. The one remaining didn't belong to me—how could it? This was the image of an older woman that looked more like my mother than me. What happened to the peaches and cream color that used to be in my cheeks? Why didn't I see when the color first began disappearing?

Does that young woman just in the mirror still exist buried in this unrecognizable face, now crisscrossed with many unwanted lines? When I smile, she does peek out, but each time I frown, she vanishes. It's as if she slipped away in the dark of night without my knowing, without my seeing, even though I was always looking. I was, really. Each day I looked in the mirror, so many times. But I never noticed her disappearing, day by day, year by year.

I miss that face that used to be mine. I wonder if I pay a surgeon a lot of money, can he turn back my "face clock?" But then I'll need him to do that again and again in the future, as each changing face over the years would become unrecognizable to me—like this last one did.

So maybe instead I can try to look in the face I have and appreciate what these many years have given me, not what they have taken away. What if I could see in the lines between my eyes not my disappointments over the years, but my accomplishments; in the lines around my lips, not my hurts but the product of my many years of smiles; in the puffiness under my eyes, not a sign of exhaustion but the never forgotten memories of the passions I experienced.

Mirrors can't change my view, but maybe I can by changing my point of view. Maybe then I will never need the short-term fix of the surgeon's knife. Maybe then I can always find me in my face, even when reflected against other images that used to be mine.

Otherwise, this face I now see, and the faces I will see in the future, will all too soon become unrecognizable to me in the mirror.

And when I spent so many years earning my face(s), maybe that is just something I don't want to happen.

# *THAT* NEXT STAGE

I started talking to myself. Just like that.

It began in the grocery store, not too long ago. "Toothpaste, instant coffee," I said out loud. Someone picked up their head to respond. But it was only my own attention I sought. How did this happen to me? Did this mean the beginning of the end of my "younger years" and the start of *that* next stage of my life? Why was I talking to myself? I wasn't lonely. Was it to help me remember?

Frankly, I don't recall.

This left me with the question of how one knows when you leave your "younger years" and enter *that* next stage. There is simply no official announcement. However there just might be some cues:

Like when people no longer say, "You look good" but rather "You look good for your age." Or when in response to announcing the news that you may be planning a facelift, friends no longer say, "Don't be ridiculous," but ask the name of your proposed surgeon.

It could also be when your cosmetic upkeep, maintenance, and doctors' appointments take almost as much time as a part-time job, when the first twenty minutes of your massage are spent detailing all your problem areas.

Or maybe more to the point, it's when you realize you prefer to dine at six, not because it's cheaper, but because the restaurant is less noisy; when you and your similarly aged dining companion instantly reach for reading glasses when the menu arrives; when a waiter's interruption means the permanent end of a thought; when you both can understand each other perfectly without either of you remembering the name of anything you are talking about; when the exciting subject matter of your conversation is not necessarily about your new lover but about the positive effects of your estrogen replacement.

And maybe it's just the simple fact that you can actually digest your lunch while discussing such topics as removing fat from your waist and implanting it in your butt or paralyzing the muscle between your eyes to remove age lines.

Of course, there's also those daily cues: that almost everyone reporting the news, those running the government suddenly got younger than you; and the reverse, when suddenly "older" men you had been attracted to are now simply too old to date.

But if none of the above cues you to entering *that* next stage, then what about when you find your phone in your refrigerator, your English muffins in your dresser; when you arrive in front of your closet with absolutely not the slightest idea why you are there.

On the other hand, maybe it's something else.

Just maybe it's when you really believe that if you have your health you have everything; when you are aware and very grateful when you wake up that nothing hurts; when you know a mistake will not cost you a job; when you begin to care more about who you like rather than who likes you; when you know anything bad is only temporary; when you know you can survive loss, no matter how painful.

I think my entry into *that* next stage will be official when I fully embrace and act on the realization that life ends, that each day, each moment counts, and is to be celebrated. That would, for me, be something to really talk about, even at the grocery store, even if out loud, and even if just to myself.

# LIFE GOT EASIER?

Once upon a time you could leave your house and just had to check if the stove was off and that you had your keys.

*But now:*
Did I turn off the computer?
Did I turn off the microwave?
Did I turn on my security cameras?
Did I take my cell phone?
Did I take my charger?
Did I take my iPad, maybe instead take my laptop?

Once upon a time buying cereal at the supermarket was easy with a few choices.

*But now:*
Do I want the large, medium, or small box of cereal?
Do I want the gluten free cereal?
With or without nuts?
With or without chocolate?
With nuts but no sugar?
With sugar but no fat?
With fat but no raisins?
With raisins but no sugar?

Once upon a time office work might not have been that easy but basically with your phone, writing pad, typewriter, carbon paper, and, of course Wite-Out, you could resolve most problems.

*But now:*
Do I really need to go through a hundred twenty-three emails before my 11:00 a.m. appointment?
Do I really need to act immediately on the twenty-seven emails that say urgent?
Do I really need to email my client to arrange a phone call?
If I call, which of the five telephone numbers should I use?
I forgot, does my client prefer Facetime?
Is it actually better to text my client?
Or should I just email my client what I want to say?
Maybe I should just go home.

I need a doctor for my nerves.
Once upon a time that was an easy appointment to make.

*But now:*
Should I go to urgent care?
Should I go to my primary doctor?
Should I go to one of my nine specialists?

If I go to a specialist, do I need a referral from my primary doctor?

Life got easier, didn't it?

That is simply too difficult a question to answer.

# TRAFFIC LIGHTS

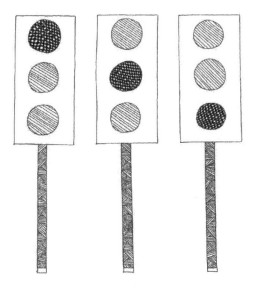

Wouldn't it be great if the choices and decisions we have to make in life were directed as simply as traffic is?

So, if you are wondering, for example, about getting involved in a new relationship, you get a *Go* signal when it is the right time to do so. You get a *Stop* signal when it isn't. You get a *Caution* signal when things are not yet certain. You will be asked to *Yield* when it is appropriate to do so. You will be told where it is OK to *Park* as a helpful reminder of your need to do just that, rest, and even take time to think about your relationship.

Yes, it would be great if life's choices and decisions came with these automatic timed alerts. But they don't. Instead you must rely solely on your internal guidance system, the one that every second of every day unrelentingly moves you, slows you down, stops you, and ultimately, if it's the system based on your own experience, takes you to your desired destination.

Then again, how can one's own guidance system take you anywhere else, as long as it's truly your own that is directing the "traffic" of your life, and as long as it's you, and you alone, in the driver's seat.

# FIGHTING GRAVITY

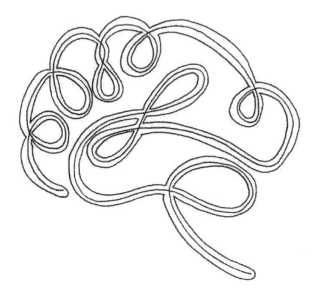

I recently heard that our brain spends approximately 90 percent of its energy on just fighting gravity and keeping us up straight.

So if that is true:

Why after being on this Earth for so many decades
am I no longer standing up straight?
Why am I getting shorter the longer I am standing?

Other things I don't understand:

Why are my ears getting longer when they hear less?

Maybe worse, why in the past ten years has no man asked me to marry him except my trainer, who is even shorter than me and needs a green card?

I guess the answer to each question is:

I am just very lucky.

That after all these many, many years of standing, the fact is I am still standing and while I stand closer to the ground, I now know the ground on which I stand.

As to my ears, the longer they are, the less they hear, the more I understand.

As to marriage, while no eligible man has proposed to me in ten years, I better understand what love is and can choose to "marry" anything in my life that brings me that love, which I learned need not only be through a man.

So let my brain keep working 90 percent in its constant fight against gravity. Along with the remaining 10 percent, it's obviously working just fine.

# DELETE

Delete. That's what my brain did with the phone numbers of the man I loved but no longer see. Should it also now delete the memories of our year together that still haunt me?

How could it have happened that we're apart? Why can't I download the whole year, press Restart, undo the ending, and restore what we had at the beginning? If so, could we then turn a redo of our year together into something lasting rather than a saved version of what we had?

Our opening was great. I still save as happiness the way we looked at each other when we first met. I still save as joy each time our toes touched before we fell asleep. I felt at home with him. I still want to save everything about those first few months. I never thought we would end.

Then things shifted. We waited too long to track our changes. We went backward, not forward. We became auto correct and stopped feeling. We began loading up on each other's defaults, not highlights. We kept tabs on our hurts and started the cat and mouse game that led us to disconnect. In the end, it was too late to pause. Each of us sought an escape.

I wish we could have edited what happened and cut and pasted the best of our times together and deleted the rest. I wish when things started going bad, we could have pressed a button and opened up a new page rather than turn our page down.

But we couldn't find the right tools to do that. While the handwriting was on the wall only months after we met, we chose not to view it. Our personal settings, background, even our favorites, differed enormously. There was no font button to press to change our script. If there was a window of opportunity for resolution, we missed it. Ultimately, we had to remove each other from our friend list, even our address book. Our chat room had to be closed for good.

I do not want to delete or trash any of the memories of that year, not even the bad ones. Rather than haunt me, I will use them to upgrade my program, change my settings of seeking a 100 percent. I will use them to remind me to zoom in at the beginning and customize, maximize, make bold those things that are most important and minimize, maybe even erase those that aren't. I will use them to seek help at the start, when it is always available, and put on the screen the remedies before it is too late.

Mostly, I will use those memories to turn my soft drive into a hard drive for a loving, satisfying relationship. To do that, I might need to freeze my system for a while, so when I press Restart, I can turn a blank page and not make a future relationship a copy of this last one with just a change of character. Then maybe I will really be online for a man to love.

# JUST YESTERDAY

J ust yesterday I woke up. I felt young.
The sun was out.
I had hopes.
I had dreams.
I had passions.

Today I woke up. I felt old.

It was raining.
I didn't look forward to anything.
Men's glances didn't stir me.
A soulful movie didn't make me cry.

So tomorrow, what do I do?

Tomorrow I will find the sun, rain or shine.
Tomorrow I will choose to be young.

# ON BEING MARRIED

Our relationship started about twenty-five years ago. Before long I said, "I do" with excitement right from the beginning. Any moment I would get a call and soon be off to Paris, London, LA, first-class all the way. Beautiful hotel rooms, great dinners at the world's best restaurants, stimulating conversations day and night. This relationship even elevated my status among my friends.

Truth and affection were not in abundance. I was mature enough to know that you can't get everything in a relationship. So even with those limitations, even when times were bad, I was so busy I didn't have much time to think. The options I was granted each and every year simply by staying connected were too good to lose.

Focused on the positive, I stayed faithful, year after year after year.

Then one day, out of the blue, and many years into it, I was told our relationship was over. As simple as that. No warning. I was no longer wanted. No longer needed. I was being replaced. Later I discovered, by somebody much younger.

What did I learn from this?

No matter how much I might be begged, no matter how many options that are dangled before me, no matter how many first-class trips I am offered, I will never ever get married to a company again.

# WHAT IF?

What if you turned left as opposed to right?

What if you woke up twenty minutes earlier and reached the corner sooner?

What if you married the man in college who asked rather than wait for the man who didn't?

What if you sold your stock when it was high rather than when the company went bankrupt?

But more to the point—your point:

What if your mother's great-great grandfather and your father's great-great grandfather didn't meet your great-great grandmothers?

And what if your mother wasn't at the party that your father attended?

Then what if you weren't here to ask:

*What if?*

# A TEMPORARY LIFE?

I s this you?

You *put off* renovating your apartment because you think you will move...one day.

You *put off* vacations hoping you will have more money, more time for an even better vacation...someday.

You *put off* buying the dress you love because you think it might go on sale...the next day.

You *put off* fully enjoying yourself on a date because you think it's not going to be a permanent relationship...any day.

If this is you, do you put things off because...you think things in your life will be different, or feel more permanent sometime in the future?

Well maybe that could be true, but I have found everything put off is lost in that time.

That however "temporary" anything feels, it's "permanent" for as long as that time lasts.

To think otherwise is to live with less than what you want and deserve even if just on a temporary basis.

Especially since "temporary" can last so long it might even feel or become permanent.

# HOW COME?

How come when I became head of a division at my company, friends said that was "nice," but when I began dating a very wealthy man those same friends congratulated me?

How come when I got a very big raise and bonus from my company, friends said that was "nice," but when I spent a week in Paris as my rich boyfriend's guest, those same friends congratulated me?

How come being a successful business woman is "nice," but to many, being the girlfriend of a successful businessman is even "nicer"?

I am not sure, and truthfully, I ask myself, "How come it doesn't really matter what anyone else thinks?"

# ON BEING GRADED

Remember the days when you were very young, when you were tested and then graded with marks at school. Good or bad, you always knew where you stood against your classmates.

Remember the days when you applied to colleges, maybe grad schools, or for employment. Good or bad you always knew where you stood against your competition.

But what happens in later years when you don't get tests and grades for various subjects and may no longer be applying to schools or seeking employment? Your tests, that happily require little preparation, might be more for your blood pressure, cholesterol, heart functioning with your only competition your last year's results. And your "applications" might be more for such pleasurable things as passports.

A definite good thing about getting older. You don't need to have a mark or an acceptance letter to tell you how you're doing against your competition, or anyone else. That no longer matters. Now you only need to do well against yourself based on your own grading system, the only system that counts. And if you are doing well against your system, for that alone, you should get an A++.

# A STITCH IN TIME

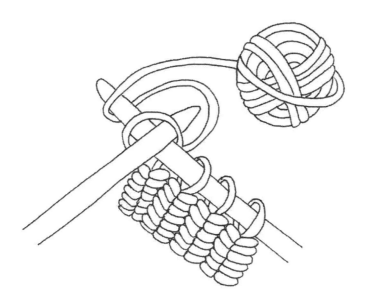

I felt like I was sitting on pins and needles, waiting for the phone to ring. I thought I might soon unravel. Would he tell me he'd left his wife—this man I thought was so perfectly tailored to my wants and needs—this very funny man who could keep me in stitches

My stomach felt like it was tied up in knots. I sipped wine to unwind. I got more wound up. Finally, the phone rang. It was he. At first, he had difficulty unbuttoning his lips. He no longer sounded smooth as silk. When he finally started speaking, he talked so fast he kept losing the thread of his conversation. I kept asking, "Did you tell her, did you tell her as you promised?" He became so silent you could hear a pin drop.

Finally, he said, "No, no, it was just not the fitting time." He promised it would be in just "another week," that same "another week" he'd promised for almost the entire six months we were together.

Did he really think I was so wrapped around his finger he could continue to pull the wool over my eyes? Maybe he just wasn't the man. I fashioned him to be. I did needle him at first before I shortened the conversation by telling him we were finished. Then I just had to hang up the phone

The fact is, an affair like this doesn't and never did suit me even though we seemed to fit so well together. It was never my pattern to be in such a relationship. Now after this call I could no longer skirt around the issue of staying the other woman and hiding him in my closet.

Too bad. I would have given him the shirt off my back if things were otherwise. But I would have to be a pinhead if I allowed myself to continue living this dream for just "one more week." There was just no other spin on this matter.

The fact is I am too fine a quality to be second to any other woman. The fact is I am no Second Hand Rose. I deserve the top of the line. Had I abided by the wise adage "A stitch in time saves nine" I would have ended this affair much earlier and it would have been a lot easier.

But casting him off after this call, even if difficult, does feel really good as I begin to design and very carefully stitch another life for myself.

# CHANGING LANES

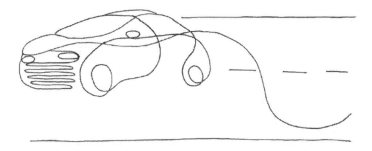

I am moving in the fast lane. I will no longer let roadblocks or stop signs slow me down. I may be passing people who care about me to get to an unknown destination. But if I don't drive myself forward, I may stall, or worse, go in Reverse and become out of style or become an old model of myself.

I have been asleep at the wheel too long. I applied the brakes so many times, they squeak. I no longer can stay in Park or continue to U-turn. I can no longer play the part of a machine while others press my buttons. I must shift gears so as not to get tied up in any more bottlenecks.

I know that I may crash along the way but that will just have to be the price to pay for change. I've signaled to those who love me my need to steer my own course and change lanes.

So fasten your seat belt—or should I say mine? I am now the one in the driver's seat. I am all gassed up for the journey.

My life is not leased from my parents, lovers, friends, or employers. I own it clean and clear. I have some dents. My finish is not always highly polished. But I have the license to be free. I earned it. More important, I give myself the permit.

No longer will I, nor can I, be the passenger. I am headed uphill. I will yield to only those whom I choose.

I choose now to drive on the freeway. I choose to stop paying the tolls for a life that was not entirely my own.

# MADE OF CLAY

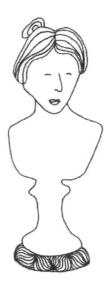

Created two years ago, I am my creator's alter ego. I've been told I am rather attractive, even though I have a few features out of place, very droopy breasts, and no body beneath them.

As imperfect as I may be, I have not aged a day in these years—a definite advantage of being inanimate—and will continue to look exactly the same for eternity, or until the moment someone decides to destroy me or accidently knocks me over. I try not to worry about things like that.

For that matter I try not to worry about anything. That's what keeps me young-looking. I choose instead to sit on my comfortable stand looking straight into my creator's living room observing her life and those of her guests. I don't do this in isolation.

Within a year of my arrival, I was joined by a lovely younger woman who, unlike me, was given an entire body. Good thing I'm not the jealous type. While I must sit up all the time, and do it on my chest, she is totally unclothed and lucky enough to lie on her back. She has remained in that position since her arrival, and I believe will forever, until she too is destroyed or accidently knocked over. Get this—she even gets a water view when the curtains are opened.

There's also a somewhat older man who arrived shortly after the younger woman, who sits on the coffee table. He's in our view as we are in his. We really don't mind sharing the space with him. He has no body, is missing the back of his head, and like us, doesn't breathe. But he has lots of hair on the front of his face, so rare in older men, and he has a strong and intelligent look though he obviously thinks of nothing.

After all these introductions you might want to know what it feels like to be a sculpture made of clay. Well, as I said, there are no aging issues. We have no lines—well, only the ones we were given at creation. We don't frown or cry, but then again, we don't smile. There are no crises about who we are, that kind of stuff. We are just what we were made to be. We can't break out of our mold. We don't even try. But we are very strong, our surfaces are unbreakable.

There must be something positive about being who we are because a number of our creator's guests, and our creator herself, at times, attempt to emulate us. They build surfaces, not unlike ours—impenetrable barriers, behind which it seems they attempt to hide themselves. It's not that hard to build walls. You simply take no nourishment, and soon you dry up and become hard.

That's what happened to us.

34

At first, we were soft and pliable and could have turned out to be anything. But we became what we are by first being molded to our creator's wishes. When she was satisfied with who we'd become (even though we might not have been) she left us alone without water or any other nourishment until we dried up.

That was our destiny—to dry up and become hard to the core. That is ultimately what happens when you get no nourishment. Don't get me wrong. We're grateful to our creator for our existence and know she did the best she could with what she knew at the time. I even forgive her for my not being beautiful.

Why people, real people, who unlike us have a choice about their destiny, choose ours is incomprehensible. Perhaps they simply seek to avoid the risk of bad feelings. If we could only tell them, if they only knew, the price of not feeling at all—how cold it is when you become hard at your core—how suffocating and confining it is to be encased in surfaces you can't break through—they'd stop building walls against feelings, stop numbing themselves with drugs and drink when feelings do penetrate. But what do we know—we're only sculptures made of clay.

Sadly, we can't tell them. We even have problems communicating among ourselves. My creator has left my woman cohort facing the river for so long she now has only one view and is noncommunicative. As to my male companion, he has absolutely no idea what I'm talking about—walls, feelings—to him that's all gibberish. Maybe that's because he's missing half his head or maybe he just wants to act macho.

So I must ponder these thoughts on my own. I have to tell you that there's some hope for the future. My creator is remodeling herself and at work again sculpting with clay. Who knows who my next roommate(s) will be?

# CONCEALED

Do I put on too much concealer, so I can't be seen even to my-self? Do I put the real me in shadow, and highlight a person I believe others want to see? Do I color everything about me to obtain outside approval? Am I too quick to gloss over what is important to me to please and be accepted by others?

Did I forget my roots? What foundation do I stand on if I am always in a rush for recognition from others? Do I create a makeover each day for others, and then not really be present as me? Is this condition of teas-ing others to believe I am who they want, permanent?

I must, I will, straighten out my priorities and brush off this need for outside approval. I must, I will, stop browbeating or lashing out at myself for what I am not, and appreciate what it is I am.

I want to be natural, not made-up. I have the formula to do that. After all, the long and short of it is that if I peel off my "mask," I am really OK just the way I am. Most important, it is only my look on the matter that really counts.

# BECOMING AN ORPHAN

I once dated a man of forty-five who said, to my utter surprise, he was an orphan. Wasn't the age limit for orphans twelve, maybe fourteen years of age?

I sadly learned that one could be an "orphan" at a much older age. I became one at fifty-three when my surviving parent, my mother, died. I vigorously fought against this unwanted title. I prayed to God daily for my mother to live, even if in a wheelchair, even if she couldn't see, even if she couldn't talk. After all, if she were to die, who was going to love me "unconditionally," protect me as only a parent is "programmed" to do. Just her existence, I pleaded to God, was enough, as with her alive I was still someone's child. I had some cushion on the generation ladder to the top of which I didn't want to climb, and certainly not that quickly.

I did not get my wish. I became, like my friend, an orphan. Soon after my mother's death, I met a woman about twenty years older than me on her way to becoming an orphan. I expressed to her my envy for all those extra years she had with her surviving parent. She responded, "Don't be, as now after all these many years having a parent, my mommy—" she still called her that "—now what do I do?"

So what does one do as an "older" orphan? There are no orphanage homes for us or adoptive or foster parents who will take us in.

I learned, I'm still learning:

To be a parent to myself.
To love myself "unconditionally" even when I fail.
To know when I am in harm's way and how to protect myself against it.

By doing this, I learned, I'm still learning:

While I have the official title "orphan," I need not feel like one.
While I am no longer anyone's child, I no longer need to be a child.
While I may have moved up the generation ladder quicker than I wanted, I still have a very long way to go.

And with feeling my parents' love and protection inside me, that climb to the top just won't be that hard or that lonely.

# INTEGRITY

I want a man with integrity. He wants a woman who is fifty. I lied about my age. If he can't trust me, can I trust him?

What is truth? Children are always truthful, sometimes painfully so. They are cute and can be forgiven. I am no longer seven years of age and no longer cute. What would I be able to get away with if I told a friend I hated her haircut, if I told a new lover that he was not as good as my last?

I have no idea as I never will. I don't take any chances. I don't want to be left alone with little else than my veracity. So I color the truth. A friend's bad haircut is always "interesting." A second-rate lover is always "different."

Recently I bought a new gown. My friend said it was quite "unusual." Does she like it? Truthfully, I don't know.

# RECIPE FOR A FULL LIFE

It seems as if it were just yesterday that men treated me as if I were a hot tomato. I was in my prime, a real dish, no longer just as sweet as honey and no longer stuck with men who were eggheads or shrimps.

That happened when my low-fat string-bean body suddenly changed and looked ready for harvest. It was a piece of cake for me to get dates every night of the week with Grade-A men. I felt like the toast of the town. While some men fed me lines, most of which were fishy, and while others treated me as if I were a piece of meat, I ate it all up, so starved was I for male adoration.

But then everything changed.

Why didn't anyone tell me that the shelf life for my youthful appearance was so short, that it had an early expiration date?

Almost overnight my peaches and cream complexion began to look more like dried-up prunes. But it was when dimples appeared on my buns and my thin thighs looked more like cottage cheese that my phone began to ring less and less and very few reservations were being made for my company. I felt as if cold water were thrown on my face. I went from feeling crabby to going nuts.

Did men think that aging meant becoming frigid and I should be put on ice? Quite the contrary. I, like most women, ripen with age into real womanliness and am sexier than ever.

Why can't they see that? I never let salt-and-pepper hair, or a pear-shape body sour me on the man. That was because to me it was never the outer layer that whetted my appetite but rather what was at his core when I peeled away those layers. The topping, even if rich, could be tempting but was never satisfying.

But I can't waste my time crying over spilt milk. My tonic will not be to whine over what is happening or tie myself up into a pretzel waiting for the phone to ring. Rather, I must begin to really relish who I am, independent of a man's taste, and wait, no matter how long it takes, for a man who can savor who I am, whether lean or meaty.

Until I find such a man, I must mellow out, and make sure to fill my plate each day with people and things I love. This is something I will digest not so much as food for thought but rather as a recipe for a rich and full life. When he comes, the right man, it will be my "just deserts" in only the best sense of that meaning. And how good that will be.

# PERSPECTIVE

Every morning, my friend wakes up grateful to be alive. Me? I wake up every morning wanting to kill myself.

My friend is battling cancer, for the third time. I am battling greed, for the first time.

I call my friend to give her love and support. I hang up the phone feeling supported.

My friend hungers for life.
I hunger for the money I lost in the stock market.

My friend feels full and vibrant when she sees the sun.
I feel empty and remorseful when I see my stock statement.

What happened to my friend was beyond her control.
What happened to me wasn't.

My friend takes chemotherapy to cure her illness.
I take wine.

Where did I lose my way?

Did my stock account become the measure of my self-esteem?
My lover?

How else to explain my insatiable appetite for more and more
when I had enough?

My friend's will to live may let her survive.
My anger, left unchecked, will kill me.

Can I learn from her?
She would spend every cent she had to be healthy like me.

Wake up, wake up, she says, the sun is out.
Cheer up, cheer up, she says,
The rain might be out, the storm might be out,
But who cares, she says,
You are able and free to go out
With or without your money.

I must listen to my friend.
"Be glad, be grateful, not mad, not hateful."

I will, please God, I will, I am—listening to you, my friend.

Thank you.

# DOWNGRADED

Say you had a prestigious job at a major company. Then you become unemployed. Are you less valuable?

Say you had a very eligible, good-looking, rich man who cared deeply for you. Then he is gone. Can your accomplishments as a woman be valued separate from being part of a powerful man?

Can one's self-worth be measured as mercurially as a stock? One day you're on everyone's "buy" list, the next day there's a correction and you become a "trade" or worse a "sell."

Do you get a downgrade if someone is angry with you, leaves you, or do you just feel worthless? Did you get a downgrade when as a child you received a C in history? Did you get an outperform when you received an A+ in another test or were you just a hold awaiting the next mark? Did your value go up when the glee club accepted you? Did it go down when no one asked you to the senior prom?

On days when you're on everyone's recommend list for whatever reason, do you parcel out shares of yourself all over the place, with little sense of your whole? Do you separate parts of yourself to please others? Does that make you feel more or less valuable? Do you think your many roles add up to more value than you as a whole?

Do you worry what your value will become when some of your parts slow down, close down, and you no longer want or are able to perform all your many roles? Will you worry about being able to market yourself again in every area of life? Do you worry who would put stock in you then? Would you think you would become a sell, or a write-off?

The answer is "no" if you do your own inventory and you stay the sole judge of your own intrinsic value. After all, who has the most "inside information" as to what your assets really are at any stage of your life? If you remain victim to the whims of outside analysts who are only long on short-term thinking, then your sense of self-esteem will fluctuate as wildly as the Dow, then you can lose yourself. That loss is simply one none of us can afford.

# GUILTY OR INNOCENT?

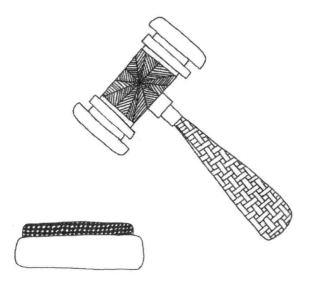

The facts have been presented. The trial is over. I am the defendant and, in this case, also the judge and the jury. I am considering a guilty plea but first I would like to deliver my closing argument. I will try to be brief.

Here are some of my "crimes." I have caused pain to others. This is not hearsay. It is a fact. I left men who loved me. I hurt people I cared for and others I courted. I left my parents' home to find my own. I hurt friends at times when their interests conflicted with mine. I swear I felt bad each time I committed any of these acts. At times I had trouble finding an alibi.

Some of the people I hurt felt damaged. They told me so. Some damage was real, some, in my view, was speculative. A number of them put me on trial for my behavior. I could not always make complete restitution, no matter how hard I tried.

Then again, there is another side. People who loved me have hurt me as well. I was counseled that "this is life." But does that give me standing to hurt back? This can't be a test case. In my opinion hurting someone is never justified. This may be an error and worth reconsideration. There really might be extenuating circumstances. I am not attempting to wiggle out of a possible guilty plea but maybe at times putting one's interest above another's is the only way to protect oneself.

That is, shouldn't each of us consider ourselves first when necessary, even if at times it's at the expense of someone else? Otherwise, each of us is at risk of becoming a public servant in jeopardy of losing our identity. As for me, I feel penalized when I lose someone I care about. But if I continue to lose myself in continuous service of others, as I (and many of us do) I will feel imprisoned for the rest of my life.

So in conclusion, and weighing the conflicting equities, I will plead not guilty and give myself a full pardon for time served. The only crime is not being true to oneself, even if others might be hurt. That has to be the rule of reason for all of us to live by, including me. And there should be no penalty for that.

# THE FABRIC OF YOUR LIFE

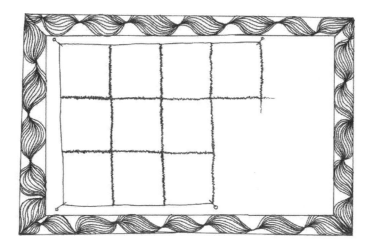

Imagine your life as a fabric.

Frame and hang it on a wall.

Is it a quilt, a mosaic of separate pieces representing maybe many loves, many jobs, even many homes sewn together by the thread of the memories you alone possess?

Or do you see a pure single stretch of silk with no seams, representing instead maybe just one love, one job, one home?

What happens if the design you once fancied may have been right in the past but today feels wrong?

How do you reframe your life? Where do you find the patches to cover what now is not your preferred design for living?

Perhaps all this is not about patching or covering anything, but instead appreciating the beauty of what was, and now making room on that same wall for what will be.

# UPGRADED

I felt upgraded today. I was offered a job. It was put to me in a phone call. What a relief. I had been in a real panic. Within the past year my company downsized. My position was eliminated. Now suddenly someone is putting stock in me again. My expertise is being sought and options closed to me just yesterday are now available. In short, I don't have to split, leave town, and sell my home. At least not now.

What does this mean? Am I worth more? Do I have more value because I have a new position? If so, what do I need to do to secure my future?

Is it simply to outperform on my job, merge myself into my new company, bankrupt my life, and be available 24/7? I did all of that before.

That was my ten-year plan. While that got me a long-term position, the sad thing was, I was so heavily invested in my work, my life was not diversified. If there was real value left for me at the end of my workday, I didn't share in it.

I did say yes to my new assignment and am happy for it. I will not, however, like before, yield to each of my new employer's demands. I no longer place any face value on the fact that it will last.

The more important fact is that I will last, whether or not employed. It is for that reason, and that reason alone, I will always be bullish on my future.

# NEW LEASE ON LIFE

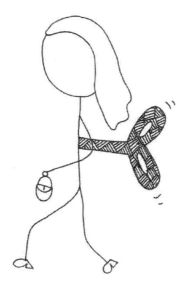

I just got a new "lease" on life. I was surprised. I never knew I was living under an expiring one. I actually was living my life as if I owned it. But out of the clear blue sky, one day I started gasping for breath, having swallowed the wrong way, and if not for the quick action of a few friends, my "tenancy" was about to expire.

It didn't, and I said "Thank God" not contemplating that I might be thanking my landlord. But how do I live under this "new lease," now that I really know I have one? It is not easy to figure out. Like the last lease, no terms are specified. Most important, it is silent as to the expiration date and the conditions for further extensions, if any.

I sought advice from other "leaseholders." Those that didn't experience a renewal as I did, offered little good advice. But those who were aware of their leaseholds, told me to constantly be aware of mine, to occupy my space for as long as I had it, with as much joy, passion, excitement, and adventure as possible, so when my "lease" comes up again, as this type of lease will do, renewal would be sought as a gift, not a necessity.

# SLOWING DOWN TIME

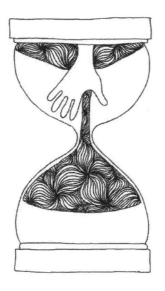

W hy does a morning, an afternoon, an evening have a nice lei-
surely pace, but a week goes by as fast as a day, a month goes
by as fast as a week, and a year goes by as fast as a month?
And each year time seems to go faster and faster than the one before—
like a roller coaster going down and picking up speed along the way.

Is it just simply that time goes faster the more time you are alive? That
is, when you celebrate your second birthday, you actually have doubled
your time on Earth. Not so when you celebrate your sixtieth, when that
year is just one-sixtieth of your time on Earth.

Even if that is true, wouldn't it be great if there's a way to make time at least feel like it lasts longer during the experience of it? Like when brushing your teeth with a two-minute automatic toothbrush. Or when you are feeling bored, lonesome, alone, scared, or worse when you are sick. Each of those times can feel endless. But who would choose any of those times to slow down the feel of the passage of it?

Maybe it's just better to feel time going fast, very fast, sometimes too fast, like when making love, listening to beautiful music, having fun. In short, celebrating life.

I will choose time to go fast, very fast, if I can fill it day by day, year by year, hopefully many years, celebrating the joy of just having it, and in that process making sure not to waste one precious second of it, one precious moment of it, one precious day or year of it regretting the quickness of its passage.

# WASHING THAT MAN RIGHT OUT OF MY HAIR

How do you remove someone from your heart after you fell head over heels in love with him?

How can you put that person at arm's length when he knocked you off your feet when you first met him, and you never really landed since?

How can you let that man go when you spent years keeping your eyes peeled for someone just like him and he finally came along, head and shoulders above any other man you met and might meet?

How do you close your eyes and forget him when months after you met you still get lost in his arms, just like the song says, when he kisses you, when he looks at you, just simply holds you, when he can still take your breath away and your heart is in your mouth when you are together?

Before I met him, I had my stomach full of relationships that went sour. Then he came along and for a while I felt that I had the world in the palm of my hand. You could have hit me over the head. I thought this time it would work. But it didn't.

What is there for me now that he is gone? Must I, can I, face it that life is not always thumbs-up?

My nosy friends have given me an earful and assure me that even if I find no one else, I will be fine alone.

But I want to feel love again.

Can I turn the other cheek and start again? Can I keep abreast of eligible men and then stop my knee-jerk reaction of dismissing them because they are not he? Is it simply a function of just making up my mind? Can I?

I must. I will soon start batting my eyes again at someone new and probably before long get my toes wet in a new relationship. Maybe to my surprise I'll be able to flip over someone again.

But not tonight. I am just not ready to put my neck out right this minute. I don't feel footloose and fancy-free. Not yet.

I need more time to wash this man right out of my hair. I will soon, I will, I must, and I promise, cross my heart, but just not tonight.

Tonight, I still only have eyes for him.

# TIME

I am Time. Mr. Webster has many definitions of me, but the fact is they are inadequate to describe me totally. I simply can't be pinned down. After all, no matter what, I keep marching on.

Some of you try to control me; others have taken courses to better manage me. Some of you simply try to forget me and are at times successful, particularly when you are making love, creating art, listening to music. Then there are some of you that try to reverse the ravages caused by me through facelifts, breast lifts, other lifts. But whether you lift anything more than your spirit, I ultimately catch up with you.

Believe me, I don't mean to be your enemy. If it makes you feel better you should know that it is not always easy to be me, to be always the same, to have nothing spontaneous happen, to never be surprised, to know where I am at every decimal of each second of a day—that is not something any of you would seek. Then again, I am never out of breath as many of you are in marching to me. I know my time always, my place in life, and I adjust for it, to it, and don't try to change it.

Why many of you are still trying to control me is hard to understand. I move at the same pace each day, every day, year after year. You should know how to deal with me by now. Yet, most of you don't seem to have time to deal with me. You are always complaining that there is not enough of me. Then when I am there, you frequently treat me with a lack of respect. Truthfully, if you would just go a little slower and appreciate me more, you might find me friendlier.

True, I come with some downsides, but look at what I provide. I gave you lots of me after your birth, for your adolescence, your adulthood. I am willing now to give you more of me for your old age. I am truly a gift. You will certainly appreciate that when I am no longer around. So if you don't appreciate me for what I give you each and every day, and you keep complaining for what I don't provide, then I suggest this might be the best time in your life to change.

# TO BE OR NOT TO BE

*On being unmarried*
O I rejoice in my independence.
I rejoice in my alone time.
I rejoice.

*On being married*
I rejoice in having someone to make decisions with me, for me.
I rejoice in our togetherness.
I rejoice.

*On being unmarried*
I rejoice in not having to sleep or have sex with the same man week after week, year after year, even if I have to make myself look good to entice new lovers.
I rejoice in being able to plan trips that I alone choose.
I rejoice.

*On being married*
I rejoice in knowing I can cuddle next to and have sex with the same man week after week, year after year, no matter what I look like.
I rejoice in being able to plan trips that we both choose.
I rejoice.

*On being unmarried*
I rejoice in taking pride in my business success and making my own money.
I rejoice in getting promotions that I alone earned.
I rejoice.

*On being married*
I rejoice in being able to rely not just on my success but on my husband's as well.
I rejoice in my status as the wife of someone who gets promoted even if I too get promoted.
I rejoice.

*On being unmarried*
I rejoice in caring for and playing with other people's children and then having a lot of adult private time.
I rejoice in spending money on other people's children with plenty left for my own enjoyment.
I rejoice.

*On being married*
I rejoice in having children even if that gives me very limited
adult private time.
I rejoice in spending money in enriching my children's lives even
if it reduces money for my own enjoyment.
I rejoice.

*On being unmarried*
I simply rejoice.

*On being married*
I simply rejoice.

And who has it better? The unmarried or the married?

The unmarried one would say she does.
The married one would say she does.

And I say both are right.

# IS EVERYTHING GOOD?

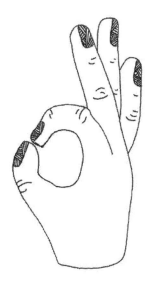

T his week:

My hair looks awful.
Maybe I should cancel my black-tie event for tonight.

I gained five pounds.
Maybe I should cancel my dinner plans for tomorrow night.

I lost a lot of money in the stock market.
Maybe I should cancel my trip to Europe.

I lost a friend. She died.
Maybe I should just stay home and cry.

*But next week:*

My hair might look good again.
Maybe I will go to a different black-tie affair.

I could lose the five pounds.
Maybe I won't need to cancel my dinner reservation.

The stock market might be up.
Maybe I will sell my stock and go on vacation.

And most important while my friend is no longer here,
I hope to be, even with my tears for her.

*So is everything good with me this week, next week?*

The fact that I had this week and will have another week, good
or bad, that is very good.

So yes, everything is good with me.

# WASTE

What is a "waste of time?"

Is loving a man, and then having that relationship come to an end a "waste of time?"

Is studying the piano and then never playing a "waste of time?"

Is getting a doctorate but then choosing to be a full-time mother a "waste of time?"

If the answer to any of these is "yes" then, does that mean that life itself, which inevitably must come to an end, is a "waste of time?"

Of course not.

So maybe nothing is a "waste of time" other than the thought that anything one cares about, even if it doesn't last, is a "waste of time."

# A PIECE OF CAKE

“*I* *am beautiful if I must say so myself. People have been work-*
*ing on me for days and days to make me look just perfect for*
*tonight. It is, after all, my coming out party. Over two hun-*
*dred people will be present to greet me and hopefully enjoy my pres-*
*ence. Maybe they will even applaud me. I will be the center of attention.*

*This party has always been my destiny. I accept that. I have a lot for*
*which I am grateful. I didn't have to do much of anything to prepare for*

*this evening. Everything was done for me or to me. I will be the star to-night. I know it. All efforts on my behalf will be rewarded. I will make everyone proud. I, myself, am proud.*

*The fact is I am not just a pretty thing. My beauty is not only on the surface. I am sweet through and through, inside and out. Don't let that fool you or bore you. I am quite complex. There are parts of me you might not notice at first glance. I have many layers, so many that sometimes it is hard to find my essence. But, when anyone will get to my core, I am quite a treat if I say so myself.*

*Enough about all this. I hear the music. This is my cue. They are coming to get me. My whole existence has been geared to this evening and I can't blow it. It is finally time. I am so nervous I could melt. I won't. Wedding cakes never do."*

If only life were so simple as it is for this wedding cake, whose purpose and destiny were predetermined, then living might be "a piece of cake."

Yet, maybe that would not be so good. We would miss the excitement of discovering our own purpose, maybe miss the rewards of breaking out of a predetermined mold created by our parents or even those made by ourselves that no longer fit.

Maybe in finding for ourselves our ever-changing purpose and destiny, we can "have our cake and eat it too." Or at the very least during our discoveries maybe our pleasures will not just be the "icing on the cake" but include the cake itself.

# PACKING

When you were young, very young,
You'd need not have worried about packing for a trip.
Your mother probably packed for you.

When you were older, but still relatively young you packed. It was fun as it included:

Sexy tops, sexy lingerie, bikinis, high-heel shoes, big sunglasses. And maybe those *happy* drugs?

When you became older, depending on how much older, packing might be a bit more thoughtful when it might include:

Loose-fitting tops, comfortable bottoms, flannel pajamas,
sneakers, flat shoes, and most important,
the *not* for *happy*, but totally necessary to not be unhappy,
*what-if* drugs taking up to maybe one third of your carry-on
items for possible back, knee, stomach problems or high or low
cholesterol, high or low blood pressure.
Plus of course, vitamins that cover almost every letter of the
alphabet.

Then the other thoughtful "essentials" to be packed:

Your hair extensions.
Your many prescription glasses for your near and
farsightedness.
Your antiaging creams for face and body.
Separate ones for your eyes, lips, neck, thighs, arms, hands,
and maybe even cuticles.
And don't forget your cosmetic bag weighing now almost as
much as your heavy shoe bag.

So is it more challenging and difficult to pack when you are older?

It might be for some but as far as I'm concerned, even if it is, it's worth
it as now that I am older:

I have the time to pack.
I have the time to take a trip.
I have the money to take that special trip.
I have the wisdom to truly appreciate every trip.

Maybe, most important to the pleasure of my trip, I can do that trip, all my trips thereafter:

*Finally, at long last,*
Totally in comfort.

# WHAT DO I MOURN?

I don't mourn my aging face as much as I mourn not knowing how good-looking it was when it wasn't aged.

I don't mourn my thinning hair as much as I mourn not appreciating it when it fell on my shoulders in abundance.

I don't mourn that I am no longer employed as much as I mourn that I spent too many hours working when I was employed.

I don't mourn spending the money on the trips I took as much as I mourn not spending more money on the trips I didn't take.

I don't mourn never marrying as much as I mourn never letting myself fully love someone I might have married.

I don't mourn the loss of my youth as much as I mourn not appreciating that I had my youth.

In the future what will I mourn most?

Wasting any more time mourning anything that was, and not fully embracing and appreciating what is, which will all too soon become what was.

# THE "NO MATTER WHAT" FRIEND

A dog can be a friend, so loyal and loving.
A cat can be a friend, so loyal, even if not so loving.
Even a goldfish can be a friend, always there when you need to see it.

And that's not counting:
A blanket can be a friend, even if it's not the one from childhood, if it gives you comfort.

For me?

I don't have a dog, cat, or goldfish.
I don't even have a blanket I can rely on for comfort.

I have to turn to the human kind,
My kind.
And I do.
And I don't have just one friend,
I have many friends.

Then, most meaningful,
To me and maybe to you,
I have my "family" of friends.

Much fewer in number, yes, but these are
The ones I can really count on.
The ones that are always there.
The ones that make me feel I'm never alone, always loved.
In short, this "family" of friends are the "no matter what" friends.

And what do I need to do in return for my family of "no matter what"
friends?

Happily, I don't need to feed them three times a day or walk
them day and night.
Instead I just need to love them and care for them in return.
In short, be to them what they are to me.
A "no matter what" friend.

And that is the friend I will always be and grateful to be.

No matter what.

# BAD VERSUS GOOD

**H**ave you ever noticed that you might talk more about the problems you had on a trip, like the plane delay or a missed connection, than about the magnificence of a beautiful church you visited? Have you ever noticed that the pain you feel when the stock market goes down is far worse and longer lasting than the pleasure you feel when it goes up?

What about watching the news? Isn't the bad news more interesting to you than the good? And might you spend more emotional time thinking of all that is missing in your life rather than appreciating all that is good in your life? Or when making a decision, might you be thinking of all the bad things that can happen rather than focusing on all the good things that can happen?

Science indicates that this is not really our fault. For evolutionary survival reasons the brain knows to separate positive and negative information and emotions into different hemispheres. It takes more time focusing on the negative to make it longer lasting and remembered better. This is genetically designed to prevent us, our forefathers, from making the same mistake twice. So next time, perhaps we will know to schedule a longer time interval between planes.

All that might be good brain work, but what is it about the same brain that is more likely to accept negative comments about us rather than positive ones.

Why is a compliment fleeting, but an insult long lasting?

Why if four friends say they love your new haircut, but one doesn't, you might want to go back to the beauty salon?

Does our brain really think that we will make better decisions if we have a bad image of ourselves?

More basic, how bad would it really be to make the same mistake twice if the gain is to savor pleasures in a deeper way?

So maybe when we recall our trips, we should take many moments picturing in our minds all the beautiful things we saw and experienced. When someone gives us a compliment, we should take many moments celebrating it.

Maybe then, memories of these happy moments can become as long lasting, if not longer lasting, then memories of the negative ones.

Even if remembering these better times doesn't help us make better decisions, they will certainly help us have happier lives.

And maybe just these thoughts could linger for many moments in our minds and go into long lasting memory.

# A SENSE OF OUR SENSES

Wouldn't it be great,
       Even if only at times,

To see like an artist might,
The varying shades of gray and black on the streets you walk,
Rather than see only the dirty footprints.

To hear like a musician might,
The rain hitting the pavement, the birds chirping,
Rather than hear only the loud honk of the car horns.

To smell like a perfumer might,
The coffee, the pizza emanating from the shops you pass,
Rather than smell only the garbage left on the sidewalks.

To touch and feel like a seamstress might,
The silkiness of a blouse on your arm, the smoothness of leather
on your thigh,
Rather than touch and feel only the roughness of an itchy part
of the garment.

To taste like a chef might,
The complex taste even in a simple piece of bread,
Rather than taste only the varied ingredients in the main
course.

One need not be an artist or expert to appreciate the gift of any
of these,
Our five senses.

The only thing needed
Is the sense to be aware of that gift and to use it,
Even if only at times.

# PICTURE-PERFECT

Life was picture-perfect. If there had been an art of living program, I would have earned my doctorate. I had a very eligible man in love with me, me with him. My hard work earned me enough money, so I didn't have to work anymore. My life was truly a bowl of cherries. It would never be described as a still life. I loved it.

But that was then. How fast life can change, even when that's not what you want. I certainly didn't. My relationship ended. I distorted my view finder, lost my perspective, made foolish investment decisions and lost a lot of my hard-earned money.

So once again back to the drawing board as I figure out what next portrait of me to paint. Too bad, I loved this last one and thought—I hoped—I would only need to do occasional touch ups.

But I can't brush away what happened, nor erase the pains. Most important, I can't be negative. All that would give me is an unwanted blank look. The fact is, I earned my expression. So instead, going forward, I must draw upon my strengths. While doing so, I will need to make some decisions:

What new life to line up on the page?
In what intensity to live it?
What values to rely on and have guide me?
What boundaries, if any, to set?

As to the background color, no question, red for passion. And I will use blue sparingly as I know the sadness I feel now will end. It always does.

I will soon be ready to start. Happily, I have all the necessary tools to do this. I've created and recreated myself enough times before. I even know how to mold myself into a new frame. I've done that before too, whether or not by my own choice.

As I paint this next portrait, it will help if I remember that it might take a lifetime of hard work to become the master of one's own fate. Until then, being a work in progress is still a fine piece of art to be appreciated, in any and all its forms.

And so I will appreciate me in whatever form, so long as I am the one painting my portrait.

# I WISH I LEARNED THAT IN KINDERGARTEN

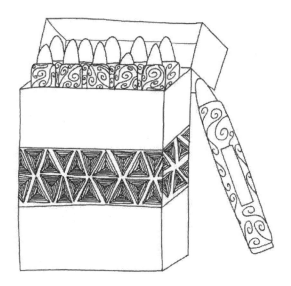

I t's OK to make a mistake.
You can always learn from it.

It's OK to fail.
At least you tried.

It's OK to love.
Even if that love is later lost.

It's OK to think of yourself first.
Nobody else might.

It's OK to waste time.
As long as you enjoy the time wasted.

It's OK to do nothing.
No one is watching.

It's OK to splurge on a dress not on sale.
You are entitled.

It's OK to eat a lot of ice cream one day.
As long as you don't do that every day.

It's OK not to be perfect.
You are perfect enough if you are you.

The only thing not OK is
To think any of the above is not OK.

# GREENER GRASS?

When I was young, like thirteen to sixteen, I was fat.
Not obese but thirty to forty pounds overweight.
I felt ugly.
I was miserable.

My grades kept going up but so did my weight.
My thin friends liked me as I would hold their pocketbooks
at dances.
They were asked to dance. I wasn't.
I suffered from overweight and jealousy in those painful

early years.

In recent years I met a woman, near my age, who tells me:
That when she was young, like thirteen to sixteen, she was
thin and beautiful.

I thought how lucky she was, gifted with what I thought
would have made me happy.
But to my utter shock she was miserable too.

Girls didn't befriend her. They were jealous of her beauty.
Boys didn't ask her out. They were intimidated by her
beauty.
And at rare times she was only a runner-up in beauty
contests.

We have both successfully and happily overcome our childhood problems. And I learned from conversations with this friend some important
lessons for "post childhood" and possible future "grass is greener" problems.

To want what someone else has is to not fully appreciate and celebrate
our own gifts. Gifts may change over time, but they are gifts, nevertheless
to embrace and not compare to others.

As to that "grass is greener" problem, I learned that the grass might not
always be greener on the other side. To think otherwise prevents us from
seeing the real beauty in the grass right in front of our eyes. That is the
grass to water and protect.

I didn't know that when I was very young. This is something I will now
never forget.

# A SUCCESSFUL WOMAN?

I chose not to marry the men who asked
So I never had the title "Mrs."
Am I a failure as a woman?

Never marrying any man who asked
I never had any children through marriage, nor did I on my own.
So I never had the title "mother."
Am I a failure as a woman?

I don't know how to cook. I hate ironing.

I don't even like to water my plants.
Responsibilities traditionally associated with women.
Am I a failure as a woman?

Instead I had a very successful career and earned great titles.
I am no longer working nor have those titles.
Am I a failure as a woman?

So I wonder—
Can I as a woman be considered successful without any title
whatsoever?

Whatever that answer is for anyone else,
I will consider myself a successful woman as my titles never
defined for me who I was or who I am.

Instead,
I am the sum total of my life decisions, which I never made
based on my sex.
Being satisfied with the results of those decisions,
I would say yes, I am a successful woman as I am fulfilled as
a person.

And to me,
that is the only real measure of success,
whatever sex,
to be satisfied with who you are.

# FOREVER YOUNG

I didn't know when I was very young that one day...
I might not be.

That all my mother's "aging" issues would become mine—and so soon.

That I would get silence instead of whistles when I walked pass a construction site.

That I might have to trade good eyesight, good hearing, and maybe some hair and even height, for more wisdom.

That I would learn that saying "yes" would be meaningless unless I also really knew how to say "no".

That I might have more freedom to do the things I wanted but less time to do them.

That I would appreciate and understand that if I have my health, I might have a lot of "problems," but if I don't have my health, I would have only one.

And what will I say twenty years from now?

That twenty years earlier I was still "very young."

That I am beyond grateful to stay "very young" as long as I continue to get older.

That I am beyond grateful for the many problems I encounter with aging as,

That means I am healthy and able to do what I want.

That I am beyond grateful that there is still so much I want to do.

So twenty years from now what will I say?

I will say I am "*Still* very young."

# BEAUTIFUL

I had my eyelashes on.
He thought my eyes were beautiful.

I had my dark reddish lipstick on.
He thought my lips were beautiful.

I had my hair extensions on.
He thought my hair was beautiful.

I had my highest open-toe high heels on.

He thought my legs were beautiful.

I had my sexy bra-lift and butt-lift on.
He thought my body was beautiful.
That night he thought all of me was beautiful.

I looked in the mirror and I thought he was right,
I am "beautiful."

After he left:

I took off my eyelashes.
I took off my lipstick.
I took off my hair extensions.
I took off my highest open-toe high heel shoes.
I took off my sexy bra-lift and butt-lift.

Then I looked in the mirror and saw Me
behind my face, and I thought
I am, just as he said, "Beautiful."

And seeing myself that way without my accoutrements
I thought, I will always be "beautiful"
Without anyone telling me.

And that to me is the only "beautiful" way to think.

# MY SISTER'S LAST GIFT

Shoulders back, stomach in, head held high—my mother's constant advice and even admonitions at times to my older sister and me—especially she would teach us this, especially when things get tough. That is, she told us lovingly when you not only had to do all this, you had to really feel it.

So years ago I threw my shoulders back further than ever, I sucked in my stomach harder than ever, I held my head higher than ever as I strolled nervously but proudly to the podium to deliver the eulogy I wrote for my older, but not yet old, sister, who at the height of her passion for life, even health (at least according to her not-so-old medical reports) learned that the slight discomfort in her side was not a pulled muscle but a cancerous liver caused by a cancerous pancreas. Who even thought about those organs?

Just yesterday, or so it seemed, we were little kids together, discovering boys together (and then wisely separately), and even discovering cigarettes and alcohol together. And in the many, many years thereafter, not once in our endless daily, maybe twice daily conversations about love, life, and the pursuit of anything and everything did words like "pancreas" or "liver" ever come up. "Heart," yes. One or the other of our hearts would be broken now and again and would become the subject of our conversation. But we knew how to help mend each other's heart. Who knew then, who knows now, not even doctors, about mending a broken pancreas, a broken liver?

Of course, lack of knowing a cure would not stop us. After all, we were sisters who could figure out anything if we worked together. My sister's job was to get well. My job was to find out how she could. She took chemotherapy until the day before she died. That very day I was still searching the internet for the cure. And while each of us failed to reach our goals, we never really failed each other as loving sisters.

But for me, still alive now, how is this possible that my only sibling isn't? My parents never told me that a sibling, my sibling, could die. Yes, they tried to prepare me for grandparents dying and they did, for themselves dying and they did, for many aunts and uncles dying, and many did, and on occasion a friend or cousin dying, and yes some did. Never, not once though, did they think of preparing me for a sibling, my only sibling, their other daughter dying—the one remaining holder of all those childhood memories, the holder of the family history, the family jokes, the hardships. I didn't think I had to ask any questions when my parents were dying. My sister and I would live well into our nineties to reminisce, or so I carelessly thought.

So now what do I do, what do any of us do when we are "sibling-less" so to speak? For me I decided it won't be with any goodbye to my sister who is still so deeply etched in my heart, soul, and mind. I must and can let go of forgotten childhood memories. I won't though let go of her teachings, which I will embrace and let guide me to my last moment. As a youngster, she taught me how to apply lipstick, how not to go all the way and still have a boy call back, let alone how to get a boy to call at all. Those were important lessons then but not now.

In that not long enough last year my sister gave me her last teachings, her last gift, maybe her best gift. She taught me with her touches, her fierce unrelenting will to live, that not only is life not to be easily surrendered, it must be inhabited fully, moment to moment, in the present. She taught me by her acceptance of her fate to say yes, not no; to not delay; to look forward, not backward; to not wait for the last minute, it will always come too soon; to not spoil one good day with tears or make one bad day worse by shedding them; and she taught so fiercely to luxuriate in the magnificence of a plain simple normal day if it is a healthy one. She would have.

And so, with my shoulders back, stomach in, head held high, so will I.

# RACING AGAINST TIME

We are all in a race against time. But this thing of living is no game. You can't play at it. Ultimately time will win. It always does. So, it is how we choose to walk through the time before the race ends that counts, how we maneuver the curves, the bumps along the way, whether we skip over what is meaningful, and whether we run away from that which we fear.

There are no rules to cover all aspects. That's what makes it so tough. We are each on our own even if we have a loyal teammate to go through all the rounds with us.

Sometimes jump-starting life again is what it takes. I did that. After kicking around for too many years, skating over difficult issues, even letting some people walk all over me, I started to reflect and take score. A coach helped me accept some of my wrong turns. The coach knew, I knew, I was never going to throw in the towel or toss away any more of my life. That's because I began really hearing the countdown and I decided to make that countdown count. I went back to the starting gate and began substituting meaning for meandering.

It is ultimately, after all, not about beating time but about getting to the finish line as a "winner" with only ourselves keeping score. And that's the kind of race I like.

# DOING NOTHING

I once read part of a book entitled *The Art of Doing Nothing*. But I couldn't relate to it.

My mother taught me early on to be always busy, always accomplish something.
She said I would then never have time to be unhappy.
My mother was very busy, very accomplished, and never unhappy.

I followed her advice all of my life.

I never had time to be unhappy.
I thought she was right.

Now, I am older, and my mother is gone.
I am no longer working.
I am busier, it seems, more than ever.
Yet somehow now I find time to be unhappy.
Ironically enough, my unhappiness is all about being so busy.

So, I start to wonder that maybe my mother's good
Advice doesn't work for me anymore.

And if it doesn't
Is there really an "art of doing nothing" that I
Don't have to work at to learn?

And maybe one day a week, or one day a month,
OK maybe every other month I could:

Sleep till noon.
Stay in my nightgown all day.
Watch old movies all day.
Listen to music all day.
Not pick up the phone all day.

In short, do nothing, accomplish nothing, all day.

At worse, if that does give me time to think, then maybe
I can think that:

Accomplishing nothing is accomplishing something.
That being idle and enjoying it doesn't mean being lazy.
It could mean being really present in the moment.
Even if it meant being lazy, I earned that right.

And at worse, if I become unhappy

Having time to think,
How unhappy can I be
If I get to watch all the old movies on my list?

# HAPPINESS

I thought when I was young:

That if I got good grades and my parents and teachers approved, I would be *happy.*

That if I was accepted into high school cheerleading and my parents approved, I would be *happy.*

That if the high school football star asked me to the prom and my parents approved, I would be *happy.*

That when I graduated high school if I got into a good college, and then into a good grad school and my parents approved, I would be *happy*.

That if I got a very good job after grad school and it paid a lot of money and my parents approved, I would be *happy*.

That all happened but I wasn't *happy* and then my parents died.

So then I thought:

That if I had a successful career that I alone achieved, I would be *happy*.

That if my monetary success could allow me to buy a beautiful apartment that I alone secured, and enabled me to travel the world, I would be *happy*.

That if I could have lovers in my life that I alone approved. I would be *happy*.

I even thought that if I could keep my weight down and knew to sell my stocks when they were high, I would be *happy*.

That all happened but I still wasn't *happy*.

So then I thought and now I think:

That my happiness can only be achieved if I choose to be *happy*.

That it can't be conditioned on the amount of money I have, the apartment I have, the trips I take, the man in my life at the moment, or with the hope that the people I love will always stay alive, stay in my life. All that can change, and the change can be overnight.

I recognized finally that happiness for me is a decision, my sole decision, and state of mind. Just those thoughts make me happy as I continue in constant excited pursuit for all the wonderful things in life that support my decision to be *happy.*

# LIVING IN THE DASH

The day we're born belongs to our parents. The day we die belongs to our mourners. What belongs to each of us is the dash—that is, what happens in between those two dates, which is the same size for everyone in the obituary columns. But how long does that length feel?

Can it feel longer if we live in the dash with great passion and purpose? Does a life consumed by envy or anger make it feel shorter? Does it matter how long or short it feels if it is filled with lots of love?

As to my dash, I passed my B. date by many years and am making my way all too quickly to my D. date. I did not live much of my dash as me. My parents lived in part of it with me, my lovers, my friends, even my employers whom I wished to please, lived in other parts.

Recently recognizing that my dash can be over in a dash, I've begun to interject myself more into it to make it solely my own. The line is feeling fuller now, and whether or not it will stretch out for a long time, I will soon be its sole inhabitant. As such, I feel very much alive and my D. date feels very far away.

And when that D. date comes, I hope the thought of fully living life in and owning ones' dash gets engraved into the hearts of all whom my dash might have touched.

# WITH NO REGRETS

**"I**t ends." What an aha moment when my friend reminded me of the Franz Kafka quote as, to him, this was the meaning of life.

I thought I became philosophical many years earlier when my sister was diagnosed with pancreatic cancer. But maybe that only gave me new meaning to the expression "when life changes on a dime". Hers certainly did. With that diagnosis there was no time for her to leave anything significant in her life undone. She didn't. This gave her strength. She could then say in the face of her death sentence, and she did say, without tears:

I have no regrets.
I saw every city I needed to see.
I accomplished what I needed to do.

And she even said in her continued celebration of life
I'm glad I just splurged on another Chanel handbag.

Well I thought if I'm to accept this most alarming, aha moment, then I wondered if I would be able to say the same things at that time. I began to think maybe it's:

Enough with cleaning my closets and apartment when they are
clean enough.
Enough with making calls to friends whose problems always
came ahead of mine.
Enough with worrying about all the many things that might
never happen.

In short, as I finally hear loud and clear what might be the true meaning of life, "it ends", I begin to think that celebrating life and doing what is significant to me, not just to others, has to be a priority on my bucket list.

I think if I abide by that, then when my day comes, I too can say what my sister said:

"I lived my life...with no regrets."

# ACKNOWLEDGMENTS

My thanks first go to my publisher, Cheryl Benton of The Three To-matoes Publishing. Tirelessly, without complaint, with unending patience and great expertise, she walked me through this new, not easy journey of being a first-time author. I wouldn't have gotten to Cheryl if not for my very dear friend Randie Levine-Miller who read some of my early pieces and said, "These should be published, send them to Cheryl!" I thank Randie for her ongoing support.

This book became a "family affair" as the beautiful illustrations accompanying each and every piece were done by my very talented grandniece, Lauren Martin who took time from her studies at NYU School of Social Work to share her talents with us as an artist. And who better than her brother, my grandnephew Todd Martin, an accomplished cinematographer, to digitize the illustrations. Then there is my artist, poet cousin-in-law, David Wainland, who unrelated to my book, wrote the poem "Just One More". What better reminder could there be to all of us, when my sister, to whom this book is dedicated, didn't have "one more". And then heartfelt thanks are due to my other family members for their never-failing support and encouragement, particularly Peter Martin and his daughter, my grandniece, Lily Martin.

There never would have been a book if not for my New School teacher Sue Rosen. It was in her writing course that I wrote many of these pieces. I thank her for waking up my right side of the brain, the creative writing side, and allowing me to put to rest for a little bit, the left side of my brain, the legal writing side that I had used for my many years in my various legal positions for Time Warner.

And with a heart full of gratitude, I give thanks to all my other very dear friends who have supported me throughout this endeavor. High on that list is Jane Shevell who provided ongoing insights and encouragement along with Stephanie Sloane and Barbara Schwerin. Also high on my list of gratitude, Geri Giddins, Judy Konigsberg, Helene Lawrence, Debbi Kusnetz, Georganne Heller, Ruth Gruhin, Judy Davis, Judi Hochman, Diane Finnerty, Sharon Ruben, Jodi Kass, Sandi Durell, Adele Abramson, Joan Kallman — and Carol Ostrow who in addition to her support also provided the subtitle of the book. Last but not least, additional thanks for the editing advice I received from Fred Wistow, Julia Coopersmith, and Sue Rosen.

I thank as well, all those friends whether named or not, who shared their life stories with me which for purposes of this book became my stories.

Abraham Lincoln was very wise when almost two hundred years ago he said "In the end it's not the years in your life that count. It's the life in your years." Franz Kafka quite a long time later said, "Anyone who keeps the ability to see beauty never grows old." So here's to all of us growing older and always seeing the beauty surrounding us.

# ABOUT THE AUTHOR

**Jane H. Goldman** is a renaissance woman. For a number of years, she was General Counsel-Vice President of Warner Bros Distributing Corporation and thereafter litigation counsel to its parent company, Time Warner Inc. She now pursues and lives her passions, which include painting, sculpting, music, and writing. In addition, she won a Drama Desk Award as associate producer of the long running show "Celebrity Autobiography", which recently had its Broadway debut. She received her BA from Barnard College and her law degree from NYU.

If you enjoyed this book, please leave a review at Amazon.

Made in the USA
Columbia, SC
19 July 2020